CAUTION TO THE WIND

CAUTION TO THE WIND

LESLEY CHOYCE

Ekstasis Editions

Canadian Cataloguing in Publication Data

Choyce, Lesley
    Caution to the wind.

    Poems
    ISBN 1-896860-72-9

        I. Title.
    Ps8555.H668C38   2000   C811'.54   C00-910489-5
    PR9199.3.C497C38   2000

© Lesley Choyce, 2000.
Cover Art: Miles Lowry

Published in 2000 by:
Ekstasis Editions Canada Ltd.   Ekstasis Editions
Box 8474, Main Postal Outlet   Box 571
Victoria, B.C. V8W 3S1   Banff, Alberta T0L 0C0

THE CANADA COUNCIL | LE CONSEIL DES ARTS
FOR THE ARTS | DU CANADA
SINCE 1957 | DEPUIS 1957

Caution to the Wind has been published with the assistance of a grant from the Canada Council and the Cultural Services Branch of British Columbia.

"You have the brush, you have your colours, you paint paradise and then you go in."
                                                    Nikos Kazantzakis

CONTENTS

Medicine Walk	9
Devil's Island On My Left	10
My Daughter, With Knots	11
Blue Beach	12
In New Jersey	13
Tafira	15
Sirocco Sky	16
Black Locusts	17
Near Oban, Scotland	18
All That's Left of Second Grade	19
Audience	20
Credentials	21
Stanley Park	22
Airports	23
Nanaimo	24
You Are The Universe	25
Trepidation	27
Two Bare Feet in Loch Ness this December	28
Silence	30
A Manicheistic Poem	31
House Call	32
Leaving New York	33
The Necropolis, Glasgow	36
Diving Among Brain Coral	37
Emotional Amnesia	39
Basic Grammar	40
The Perfect Advice	41
Toronto Airport Piano	43
Sudbury Story	44
It's a Terrible Thing	45
For William Golding	46
Winter Day at Little Gidding	47
Flying Home From England to Nova Scotia by Way of New York	48

Letter to a Friend in Ottawa	50
Reversing the Dog on the Ratchet	51
On Digging My First Well	52
January 19, 2000	53
The Death of Donut Land and Other News	54
Insomniac Pier	56
Home Improvements	57
Full Three Fathoms	58
For Women Undergoing Mastectomy	59
A Love of Old Things	60
Going Home	62
Song of Myself	63
Orion Keeps Me Honest	64
The Middle Ground	65
On the Air	66
Tornado Outside Disney World	68
A Small Sad Dog in Paris	69
At the Too Much Hotel in Ottawa	71
I've Always Been Good Friends With My Mind	72
Last Will and Testament	75

Medicine Walk

When you believe you are beyond repair
let go.
When you can not be saved by all your friends,
when you can not be saved by yourself,
forget who you are
and deliver what is left of your
to that place
you have been to before
but did not understand its worth.

Use whatever means to get close
but then you must walk the rest of the way
and if you can not walk
then crawl.
It is your only hope.
The word "sacred" could scare you off
so be silent
be there
and do not ask how
boulders covered with star moss,
wind-bowed apple branches
or the song of a small chanting brook
can salvage you
but it will.

Some very important people I know
have been saved
by the song of the smallest birds,
others redeemed by the smell of leaves rotting in a forest.
Remember this.

Devil's Island On My Left

Two winds, one north, one south,
meet here right now where I stand —
the sea, the land, the smell of each,
upon me like the working lungs of two good friends.
These shores of Lawlor's Island are good as any
to comb through the things shovelled into my head.
Who am I now?
A walker on a plastic littered shore.
How did I get here?
A kayak, yes, one filled with air,
now hidden in the arms of thick, quiet spruce.
Renaming an unwritten novel as I walk,
what else to do?
Pick up a drifting hat with one word — Caution
My great conundrum, the usual:
I've trekked this far, now what's beyond?
An island's shore will never fail
to circle back
to where you first
put foot to solid ground.

My Daughter, With Knots

My six-year-old daughter would come to me
with knots to be untied —
rope and shoelace,
string and sashes.
The mystery behind these knots, at first,
made her angry — but then she grew to understand
there's beauty in the untangling.

The knots once arrived of their own accord but now
she's older and invention is her game —
knots tighter, and more convoluted
than anything nature could conspire on its own.
And still she delivers them to me to
deconstruct
pretending the work is not her own.
It seems each day, the task is more difficult,
the untangling time grows longer,
the looped geometry more perplexing.
Ten years from now, we'll continue on
at a similar game:
two loose ends, a knot,
a hidden pattern to be followed in
to unravel the core of confusion.

BLUE BEACH
(near Hantsport, Nova Scotia)

Old dog at the end of the rutted road,
black with a comedy of grey around the mouth,
waiting for me to arrive.
She follows me down to the antediluvian shoreline
of Fundy's Minas Basin,
tide sliding out on the smooth flat stones of slate and shale.
Above me, the high graphic cliffs, strata like old books piled
on their sides, some stories more important than the rest.

A black arthritic dog on a black beach
on a warm afternoon, fossils everywhere,
walking back into the Jurassic,
the smell of buried rainforests.
After a morning of rain,
curtains of fresh water fall from mossy slopes above.
Stand behind the cascade,
your back up against the ragged cliff
and realize how far you've travelled.

Blue Beach: a poet's call
when silted water on black rock
finds that certain slant of light.
My shoes orchestrate a satisfying canticle,
a tempoed crush of thin flat stones.
I help the sea undo these walls of Fundy
as the three of us
hike back into the throat of geography
guided towards the memory
of insects adrift in a tropic rain,
of worms exploring the soft, lavish mud,
of ambitious living things sampling air,
crawling up onto the shoreline
waiting for the twenty-first century.

In New Jersey

In New Jersey
the highways keep chewing away at my father's garden
until all that's left is an isosceles of soil
where he plants some Burpee corn,
the last defence against the siege of the suburbs.

By July the tall stalks support great ears of ripening fruit
but the racoons dodge cars and tandem trucks
to pilfer as they must —
my father's corn is worth the risk of ruin on any road.
Aware that life is one long intricate defence
against everything
my father runs a wire to the field in front
and plants a radio beneath a bucket —
a small rock and roll arcade,
a galvanized pavilion of music from Philadelphia,
believing that raccoons will be offended
and seek farther fields to plunder.

The new immigrants in the neighbourhood from
Portugal and Pakistan, from Malaysia and Egypt,
watch my father arrange the small shrine
and gather later on the sidewalk
to discuss its religious implications.
All admit there are many things about this new land
that they are trying to understand.

The raccoons hold off for several days,
the kernels of corn ripening yellow and succulent,
until a human thief from farther up the road,
tempted day after day by a radio in a garden
playing hip hop and rap beneath a bucket,
steals the music from the small temple one night
and silence

(diminished only by the sound of tires sucking wet asphalt),
lures what's left of the wilderness back into the garden
to bend the stalk of green ambition and
savour sweetness never meant for human tongues.

Tafira

The donkeys on the hills above Tafira, Spain
wander the slopes
with ropes tied to their feet
front to front, back to back
another definition of freedom
without fences.

Wishing for a knife to slice the knots
my daughter and I follow
the worn trails of the gentle animals
and study thorned cactus and dry weeds
collect grey stones with green lichen
smell the tumbleweed flowers
here above Gibralter Strait.
In full daylight a white ghost of the moon
three-quarters round
hangs like a pale medallion
over Africa's northern shore
beckoning or warning.

On foreign hills
it's so hard to tell the difference.

Sirocco Sky

In Portugal is an old stone seaport
with a small dark hotel that took us in
to sleep a fitful night in a cold square room
that wreaked of insect poison.
The church bells behind our tomb rang all night
at twenty minute intervals,
loud enough to cancel all the dark Mediterranean dreams
that filled the hopeless night.

Pesetas, escudos, a kind of lukewarm cabbage soup
cloned white houses with blue tiles
and forests of cork whose bark they peeled.

Next day, in Spain, we ate at McDonalds.
Sad but true
and all the pickpockets and car thieves in Seville
were sorry
to see us leave so soon.
I can still see them,
a small army of men with operatic mustaches,
exotic troubadours, waving in the rear view mirror
as we crossed the Guadalquivir River.

Somewhere up ahead, Europe's southern shore,
windswept trees,
sand dunes like tangible cumulus clouds
anchored on earth,
solid enough to hike upon
but soft enough
to swallow our grief
as we climbed their backs
then threw ourselves high into the sirocco sky
to fall softly back to earth
on their pure white slopes.

Black Locusts

I'm thinking of old black locust trees,
wood hard as steel,
alien and deathlike in winter
when icy roads send reckless teenagers
driving their cars into the bark.
Those trees point to the cold moon
like the fingers of old angry men
in private battles with unstoppable pain.

In spring, black trees bloom into white,
a million corsages for the wind,
inside each blossom,
small gifts of seeds for migration's appetite.
In summer, the deep rutted hide of the black locust
is a highway
for earth-bound insects to storm the heavens.

The worth of such trees depends on your age.
I'm the thirteen year old boy in the second story window,
breathing the perfume of your flowers,
counting the dancers in the ballet of oval leaves
in the sunset
until I find the courage
to call her on the phone
and speak the language
rooted in my heart.

Near Oban, Scotland

It was a large round day
blue of sky and green of mossy field;
the town was quiet as a smooth, wet stone,
our eyes like glass in sacred walls.
Above the sea, the wind was cold and sweet with salt
and all around the strewn rocks sang.
The sheep remembered who we were
from former lives on higher hills.
Below, the loch was home to reeds
that hosted songs from half of Scotland's birds.

Though winter was the name of now,
a mismatched pair of word and time,
I took a gulp of highland air,
I crossed the field and closed my eyes
attempted braille on ancient rocks.
No one knew the code of runes
but fingers traced ancestral stones
and druids watched us smoothing moss
yet stayed as silent as the wood
of country crosses placed outdoors,
those Celtic relics left behind
to test the wide-eyed pilgrims.

All That's Left of Second Grade

All that's left of second grade is this:
1. Tuesday afternoon dodge ball — my feet knocked out from under me, the smell of noseblood on warm asphalt;
2. The squeal of chalk on blackboard like the sound of some innocent animal dying a hard and needless death;
3. The world outside the high window — bare tree limbs rattling ice (a "ruined choir") — the exotic language of ice and truth so near to lunch;
4. A short oral report on groundhogs — prepared well despite disappointment on the loss of killer whales to James Hanselmann;
5. Awkward moments around smart girls; how could it be they were all smart and beautiful back then?
6. Eddie Lawson throwing up on Lance Hubbs — the dark horse event of the year.
7. A bell at 2:15, a yellow bus delivering us all back into a safer world.

Audience

They want me to stop talking out loud to the stones,
a harmless discourse, I argue,
but the language of youth changes vernacular in the hours of age.
A young man's ambition
bounces off deaf ears of granite
but the solemn report of an older soul
rattles hard against the tempered rocks
along this shore.

An afternoon sun that some would see as copper
is a softer fuse to light up the volcanic refugees
here wet with winter sea.
But a human voice in a failing light
is another matter altogether.
Still, an audience is a necessary thing —
and some would say these cold boulders are easier to please,
more ready to keep an open mind,
than all the citizens of Halifax
or cities further on.

Credentials

My father shipped home from Africa
at the end of the war
by way of France
to cross the Atlantic
and prepare for the Pacific
to fight Japan
but Truman dropped a pair of bombs
Hiroshima, Nagasaki
thus freed my father from bloody tasks of state
so he could marry the woman he loved
and bring my brother and I complaining into the new world.

The odds are more than good
that I owe my existence to those incinerated in Japanese cities
by American science.
It's why I've felt I was born to fire and ash
and soon ran from urban streets where
the portraits of charred victims
seemed etched on every wall.

Stanley Park

Old growth trees, tops busted down by centuries
always a new arm growing from a skyscraper stump
saved from lumber.
Saddle-sore on a rented bike,
gravel crooning an old tune,
ravens arguing all along the route
about God and bread crumbs.
Black squirrels like attic rats on some kind of crazy jag
diving for my spokes,
marital problems in ancient cedar stumps.

Skies clear as a blue TV screen in a Granville Street store,
fingers finding all the gears,
racing home to whatever's left of civilization.

All around, the West Coast geography, bragging.

Airports

Carpets all the colour of raw sewage in a flood,
three-year-olds, working like Picasssos on the smeary windows
with sticky paws of snot and elaborate spinnakers of drool.
Airports have no sense of smell but large antiseptic minds
that run towards pillars and vents and dull grey walls.
The airport acts like a haven, though, for office men
rooting through attache cases and palming cell phones.
All airports have taken night classes in self-importance
or read the guidebook sold at Coles
on their way to a late flight for Ottawa.

Before the days of Rapidair,
farmers with failed crops
allowed planes to bounce to earth in their potato fields
and pilots walked home with grass stains on their knees.
Now the airport sends her children, all cloned,
to any place it can discover or afford.

Those anxious to avoid home can pay large sums
to sit with bored strangers
preparing for a race through the heavens to anywhere
while the sky pretends it doesn't care
and conjures clouds like dandelion flowers
gone to puffy white spheres.

Nanaimo

Once an empty patch of coast
with its own aspirations toward crags and gnarled beauty
then people came and scattered the seeds
of shopping malls and schools
gave their children asphalt, skateboards and drugs
then slipped off to the rec room to watch Letterman.
Foreign dentists arrived to steal the salmon from the beaks of eagles
then let the fish go bad in the RV fridge
on the ferry ride back to the mainland.
Movie stars buy condos here but can't afford
the time to visit
those empty husks of pinkish concrete
that stab like fingers into the sunlight of May.

The ravens who have not read Jung
fly up the island beyond Campbell River
looking for the safety of a cold damp wind.

You Are The Universe

You are the universe, you really are.
You are the entire intergalactic map and more:
you are up and down, overhead and underneath.
You are all the way to the right
and farther than my imagination can reach to the left.
You are the universe and every day is your birthday.

Every time you open your mouth it is the sound of time unfolding.
You are the outside of the envelope and the white part inside;
your favourite game is playing hide and seek with yourself
and we are watching from the sidelines.
We hear your music at night, the soft static of stars
and dance to it beneath the canopy of yourself.
Because you are the universe
and for you it's one big long vacation
with fireworks and a soundtrack.

You are the universe, nearly infinite, we're not sure,
but you are always yourself, always muddling your way through,
always dark and secret and bright and explosive because
you are the universe and some of us would like to be friends.

You are moving away from us at the same time
that we are part of you, and you are part of us
and we wonder what it must be like to be the universe even though
we are the universe, too, or a small part of it.
Some of us are arms and legs of the universe,
some of us are brain cells or finger hairs of the universe.
I've known people who are other body parts of the universe
but we're all necessary so what the heck.

Your speed is fast, breakneck,
and you think gravity is a thing to dance to.
Some of us have found comfortable homes
in the universe
on favourable planets with kindly stars
you have given us,
or ones we have borrowed.
It's all a matter of time, I understand.
Time is like the best friend of the universe.
Everything exists within time, or so we believe.
Time constantly plays the good cop bad cop game with us,
did you know that?
Of course, you knew that because you are the universe,
you are everything;
that's the role you were given when you were just young.

You are the universe and I suppose some days
it's a job like many others.
Ups and downs. We can sympathize with you
despite your size. (Enormity is the word that comes to mind.)
Deep down, though, I believe large things
are very small, or maybe simple, anyway.
Basic but somehow universal:
everything that happens matters to you since it is part of you.
You are probably not allowed to be very emotional about everything,
being the universe and all.
But I bet you are anyway, sometimes.
I bet that some things that happen to us, or to you,
make you cry.
And I can tell when you are feeling good.
Like right now.
You're feeling pretty good about all this.
Because you, you are the universe.

Trepidation

I know all about fear —
fear is the hand that holds me down
when the broken wave
swarms over me with cold December's churning sea.
It coils around my head
and wraps my legs with baling wire
and only my arms flap free like strange frantic birds.

Fear is the hand that shakes with death
and greets the deep
that wants my bones.
So often lately, you seek me out
and probably you know the trick
to turn the mind and almost win.
But when I'm sucked beneath the wave
and surface only next to find
another larger, meaner foe
I ply my trade of quiet grief
and swim direct into the throat
of smashing seas and cold regret,
then dive to depths
where calm collects
and anchors hope with simple dreams.

By when my lungs are near collapsed
and dread has gripped my neck at last
I call forth hope to swim with me
while fear gives up and hurries home,
its name inscribed inside my skull,
its thumb print blue upon my throat.

Two Bare Feet in Loch Ness this December

Head in the tenth century
one hand holding onto bark,
the advice of this gnarled tree
up to its knees in mystery.

Snow falling from a Celt's brooding sky;
the hills have their own concerns
and ignore the admonition of seasons.
Small stones flecked with mica —
plucked from the belly of the loch —
a pillage of dark mirrors
echoes of ruined swords
dismantled by the broad pacifism of time.
All of history is darkness
with small promises of cold light
like this.

The honesty of winter sings the same truth
as the moods of glaciers etched in the walls of the glen.
A dark road ahead, slick with snow
as the hills will send us down
to Inverness
but first the calligraphy
of dark ripples on empty water, luxurious as ink,
snowflakes devoured by the deep lake.

I walk to shore where my two daughters stand
laughing at my complaint.
The cold knives of sharp Scottish stones
dull quickly.
This family, the three of us,
grinning nomads of unlikely epochs,
backs braced against the failures of layered politics,
tracing the Great Glen east

down to Findhorn
the North Sea
and a single lonely stone, a story,
left in a field by the Picts
waiting for us at daybreak.

Silence

there's really no point
in speaking
if you can't improve upon silence
unless, of course
silence needs a foil, a frame
and that's our only roll
fine fretwork
around something perfect
and empty

silence is always welcome to grow as large
as its unique weight will allow
but we will always want
to attempt improvements
on its borders
with all the confusion
we can muster

A Manicheistic Poem

Death
ice drips
silver needles
from the eyes of darkness.

Life
blind sun bursts
gold against the dark,
pours yellow
lawn
over the night,
melts
sharp horror back to
benign
wet reason.

House Call

Good morning,
I am collecting affidavits
for the inevitable
defence
of us all.
Perhaps you've been
concerned
about
the mess we're in,
the fact that
the world is unsafe,
that it wobbles
like a balloon
perched on a pin
while a thousand angels
dance on its skin.

Maybe too you've been worried
watching the news.
I know it makes me nervous
although
at night
the sky is still sometimes
comfortingly dark.
There's hope for us yet
as it remains tolerant and still
awaiting our bright graffiti.

Maybe you will consider
signing
right here.
It might help.
You never know.

Leaving New York

In May I give New York back to itself
say goodbye to the hungry mouth of the Lincoln Tunnel
and declare the city is through.

After I leave, they will tear it all down
find other things to do for the panhandlers
and prophets hawking the *Bilial News*.
The men with perfumed hair on the subway
will have to give up their briefcases
and learn to forage in the woods,
the crowds at Time Square will thin to empty streets
and the sparrows will inherit Forty-Second Street.

The city taught me well:
survive on stale air if you must,
death by city street can be avoided.
Watching a sailor outside Macy's coughing up blood
I know how painful life can be.
Measuring my thumb against the Exxon building,
I know we all are equal.

Wild Jerusalem artichoke will bloom on Broadway;
dandelion and plantain will rule the Avenue of the Americas.
But I'll never forget the rooftop ads of liquor bottles
taller than houses
painted in those smoky skies by Madison Avenue Da Vincis,
shouting those colours that insist
we must consume to live
and having consumed we will always give whatever's left
back to New York.

We sent old lies back there to die;
they'll dream away into old age in the cracks of sidewalks,
they'll wrap up in the *Daily News* and be happy.
All our failures will be there for daily reunions
near the statue of General Grant
while the Village and the Bowery will be reserved
for ambition short on change.

Some of us will miss our companions, the ones we never really knew
— the young junkie who sat beside me
while I ate liverwurst sandwiches on a bench
behind the public library.
I got used to him tightening the belt around his arm,
the slow press of the needle into the vein,
admired his casual demeanor
there beneath the statue of William Cullen Bryant,
author of *Thanatopsis*.
It's possible they will both be swallowed by the streets
before they find a way out.

As I ride the bus west, confident of the finale of New York,
I expect there will be surprises for some.
Tomorrow someone else will fill this seat headed east;
he'll be here near the back of the bus
hoping no one will sit beside him
on the thirty mile trip.
He'll crack the window slightly
and stare at the dandruff on the shoulders
of the career builder in front of him.
On his way to work he is already returning home in his mind;
the day's over except for the putting in of time.
The bus will slip into the dark tunnel and he'll rest his eyes
and when he opens them again,
he will have emerged onto the island and discovered

along with the rest
that someone has replaced the city
with a million possible avenues
into the future.

The Necropolis, Glasgow

Old rich men buried here
above the modern brewery
that bathes the city with a yeasty smell,
the occasional burst of burnt malt
conspired by a workman angry at his boss.

These graves have seen the work of diggers in the night
stealing fresh corpses for the school of medicine one year,
searching out rings and necklaces
from the elegant fermented dead
on other occasions.

The pubs of Glasgow saw many men conspire through the centuries
over dark beers
where and when to dig,
return later for a second draught
as the moon rose higher in the night
to lift a pint to health, another to the thing that steals it away
and allows a poor man a living.
Soiled hands around an amber glass,
as the sweet sickly smell of a coal fire
reminds him of one comforting thought.
He that dies of wealth is as dead as he who dies of dearth,
the only difference this:
the poor have better guarantees
to stay undisturbed
in the thin, cold soil of this bonnie land.

Diving Among Brain Coral
(*Speightstown, Barbados, 1986*)

We share this form, these dents and ridges —
you a giant among the living rocks,
me hovering above, a voyeur with my own twin hemispheres.

I am an alien here suspended
on the ceiling dome of your world
watching the dangers that lurk about in your cerebral dimension.
Anemones blossom and retreat
like adrenalin ideas
imagined and abandoned
and urchins (like evil thoughts)
are tucked beneath your lobes
and if I hover long enough
a moray eel will dart from fold to fold
and feign attack at the shadowy thing above
then slip back into its cranial haunt.

All morning I float here, back to the sky,
a dead man except
for the plastic pipe that feeds me air.
This odd irony that face down, a man can float for hours,
motionless, at home in the sea, but turning over
he will sink without motion.
What cruel evolutionary fate
allowed this trait?
As if to say, at sea, we are only meant to peer down
into the crowded depths
never up into the cloudless heavens.

But I am prepared to meet my mind's true mirror
on its own terms.
The water all around is warm and blue,
the worst of dangers would stalk me further out
on reefs beyond the sight of land.
Between us, the schools of animate colour
make highways
towards richer grounds
both east and west.

My blood is salt,
my feet have fins,
ancestry is all around
but below some force has borne this life
that reminds me now of something new:
we've borrowed much from every kind
some day they'll need some paying back.

Emotional Amnesia

After a while
we forget what it is like
to simply love all strangers
to love them all and forgive
even the cruel ones.

After a while we forget
the names of feelings
and make up new ones to replace them:
ivory and babilah,
moloch and sedan.

Even now the fragile emotions we fail to name
fade into light
and reason.

Language is a crude bartering of sound for meaning
approximate, inaccurate
the best we can do to give form
to so much we don't understand.

Basic Grammar

I awoke again this morning to discover
I didn't know who I was
so I curled up deep inside the language
to find new hope.
When I surfaced I felt like a verb — young, indulgent
but in the mirror discovered my face,
a noun,
pronouncing age and duty.

I refused the advice of adjectives
and grew angry at the vocabulary
that tricked me
but soon fell in love
with adverbs
moving so gracefully through the morning
that I could not resist.

Before I am prepared to face the world,
I will understand
I am only a clause,
nothing more.

The Perfect Advice
(*Dublin, 1992*)

Lost on a nameless street in Dublin,
on the way to the Guinness Brewery tour
in a neighbourhood of kids throwing rocks at all the available glass.
An old man we ask for help
leans towards the car and admits,
"You're lost but it's not hopeless,
just close to it.
It's alway that way in Dublin."
He grips two bony hands on the half rolled down window,
and like a preacher at the pulpit
he peers into the dim light inside the car,
thick glasses, reddish face,
tilts his head at my wife:
"You're married then?
Well good. I was too
but she died.
I'm alone now
but I was a very lucky man."

Half of Ireland's traffic is tied up behind us now:
propane truck, brewery workers, garbage lorries.
Anger is everywhere;
drivers' horns barking for blocks,
even the kids have stopped their
spray of stones on the vestibule glass.
He studies my own hands gripping the wheel of the MG,
pities me for driving a hired English car
but nods again at my wife,
"Hold onto her boy
don't never go to bed angry at each other
and you'll do alright,"
then taps the door and backs away,
notices the commotion he's caused,

tells the rest of Ireland to go to hell
and walks off home
to sip a single cup of tea in a rented room
that smells like 1932.

Toronto Airport Piano

Windiest morning of November,
the gales of the *Edmund Fitzgerald*
brooding wicked skies
but major sevenths in a bright room
music the colour of Nova Scotia summer
here in unlikely Toronto.
Between swollen sounds of famous arpeggios,
the leap of security alarms
begging for minor chord accompaniment.
Arrest the moment with something diminished
before rushing off to Gate Seventeen.

Sudbury Story

A certain safety in living in the place a meteor struck
even if it was a hundred thousand years ago.
And at a school near Copper Cliff,
nearly in the shadow of the Big Nickel,
a boy from grade six telling me
about the most important thing
that happened to him when he was four:
visiting a friend, he opened the storm door
and knocked loudly.
A cold north wind slammed the outside door behind
wedging him locked into that slim space between
the outer and the inner world.
With no one home and no way out, he was trapped there
for nearly an hour
till freedom found him and sent him stumbling home.

Outside Sudbury, the birch reclaim the acid hills
of black baked stone.
In early summer, the delicate pale green of leaves give soft asylum
to the Boy Scouts planting spruce;
recovery is an anthem here,
while up above the monolith cathedral spire
of the Inco stack breeds smoke
that hijacks the upper winds and speeds off east
to spread its news:
the price that's paid, the human cost
of mining wealth
from gifts from space.

It's a Terrible Thing

It's a terrible thing
to remember a place
only in terms of one thing.

Georgia for example
is a grey sticky morning at a rundown gas station
with a bathroom
that hadn't been cleaned since the Civil War
and a toilet
that wouldn't flush.

Gary, Indiana is a yellow fog on the turnpike horizon.
All of Alaska is reduced to a stolen Anchorage road sign
or the camouflage of ptarmigans on a red tundra.
Mexico is a sad row of ramshackle houses beyond the Rio Grande.
All of Wales is slag and shale, a dirty fork and bad spaghetti;
Northern Ireland a Jewish store owner near Belfast
with a daughter-doctor living in Calgary.

So much is lost in our compression,
I've lost track of almost all of continental Europe
except for a confused morning,
waking up on a train heading the wrong way
towards Russia.
The continents I've never seen
seem more complete
as if imagination
is the only honest way
to preserve what's left
of my world.

For William Golding

Back home in England, he says, he sits
in his backyard without great thoughts
playing piano in his garden
surrounded by the accompaniment of song birds,
miles and years away from *Lord of the Flies*.
He never worshipped a pighead on a stick
but as a boy (confesses now)
he fought his chaps, drew blood
and liked it
before he
discovered good and evil get easily misaligned
inside the confines of civilization.

We debate the hazards
of booze and sex
and literary immortality
and Golding confesses
he's never bothered by any of the three.
He never drinks, he's married and, as for legacy,
he'll let the sad stuffed scholars
please themselves
while he prefers to now and then sail down the Nile
on a leaky boat or chat with sods like me
or pound the keys in Cornwall
until the world's set straight
by one ambitious chorded medley of memory
and sunlight.

December Day at Little Gidding

An old man with a wheelbarrow
refusing to offer up directions without full theatre;
before he mentions a left hand turn by the hedge,
he's twelve and on his first
horse on a green pasture
with his mother fearing for his safety and him
hanging on for dear life.

As if to illustrate some consummate point,
he picks up his hoe
and holds it up with two strong brown hands.
"It was down that way, at least it was when I was a boy."
Like a literate fool, I ask if that's the place,
the small retreat, the chapel, the poem from *Four Quartets* by Eliot.
"Don't know no Eliot. Perhaps there was once.
And a chapel, yes.
Strong religion in that place.
I never believed in God till one Sunday
in there with the light through the stained glass
shining down on the ankle of a girl
along the pew.
Heaven took me then
and never gave me back."

Flying Home From England to Nova Scotia by Way of New York

Looking down from thirty thousand feet,
I imagine I can see my lake, my gravel road,
my own back yard.
"It's nice to be from somewhere,"
the woman from Pittsburgh beside me says
when I point down to home.
Her trip, her whole life, she says
has been a maze of misplotted journeys.
No one believes I can see my house
but there it is, covered with wooden shingles I nailed myself,
brown van in the driveway, a smudge of snow on the lawn.

A parachute would save me time.
Instead a woman brings plastic boxes of food
smiling a square professional smile
and then the clouds seal up Halifax
and we push on south to New York.
A man begins to argue with anyone
who will listen while hugging a small valise —
the ashes of his dead wife, he says
although most of us are convinced it's a bomb.
Pittsburgh is angry she isn't home now,
even though she's unconvinced where home is.
A storm keeps us from landing
as everyone gets more upset,
all eyes on the man hugging his dead wife with such hostility.

Eventually, the customs man in the airport asks my name
and when I tell him, he pretends to believe me.
My wife touches my elbow, assuring me that I exist.
"We're Canadians," I say,
"just flew over our home in Nova Scotia."
"You should know better," he says
and waves us on while outside
lightning divides the dark sky
between safety and the unknown.

Letter to a Friend in Ottawa

I'm working on astral projection
at night
while I sleep.
So far I can only get to the blinding white light
I call fat lightning,
might take some time to get past that and find
something more interesting

The waves I surfed
at Hockey Island yesterday had
God smiling back at me inside each perfect tube,
then snow on the big hill in the afternoon
on a plastic toboggan with my two kids
spilling out at full speed into dunes of soft white safety.

I think I'll have to find a way to whittle
the fat shaft of white light
down to a thin silver thread
before I can use it for transportation
which could prove to be too much effort
for somebody trying to sleep.
Hard to know, if it could take me any place
more perfect than here
and now.

Reversing the Dog on the Ratchet

long lost again on the afterdeck of the afterthought
below the bejesus bonsai brain,
cowering in the inferno insistence that the bark is
bolder than the tornado
spinning on the waves below the westerly winds,
soporific on one sanctimonious sandspit
sliding inside the tube at six a.m.
soldered to the wave like a
barnacle on the back of euphoria.

Twice the rider found wisdom in the
wayward afternoon, before the brogue,
born of the fastlane
sliderule in the side pocket of destiny.

Some claim to know the conundrums
rolling about the bottom of the sea,
gallons of gulf stream idioms
pondering their plight or purpose like
migrating cod caught in the nets of tomorrow.
Others speak
philosophy in the mild mists above the headland;
how often I've tried to
grab for garrulous messages from the fronds of spruce,
the nubs of
springborn fiddleheads
for no clear reason
but then nothing is certain
on the oftentide of
happenstance.

On Digging My First Well

We drank for a decade from a round hole
I dug by hand from a cleft between
knuckles of bedrock.
Against good advice, the well sustained us
because of belief more than anything
and because I kept the drillers and backhoes at bay
in favour of sweat and blister,
the creative badge of the pick axe and shovel artist.

I harvested each rock
from where the glaciers had planted them
and presented them to the sunshine of the twentieth century,
a great surprise to all invited.
Then slopped buckets of muck skyward
until you could lick the backbone of the earth,
only six foot down to bedrock really,
a tiny dent in such a deep planet.
But this land prefers to table her water at kneecap depth
so I carved a wider arc through shale and slate,
Pangaea's gift (before she drifted west to
become Africa).

The shallow spring proved faith in any worthwhile folly
and slaked our thirst,
a source so close to the backdoor's closure
that the well remained safe
within the boundary of devotion.

January 19, 2000

Old big raven in the garden
rooting around in a foot of pure white snow
beak down, head buried
burrowing like my dog
searching for summer.

When he pulls himself back up
and barks into the cold clear air
the message is clear:
it's nowhere to be found.

The Death of Donut Land and Other News

Sad history here in the gypsum hills of Hants
the new Tim Horton's off the 101
has slain Donut Land.
The clones continue to kill off all of us
who are one of a kind.
The aged and tilting chimney stack of the old textile mill in Windsor
so Italian in its angle against the summer sky
has been razed for safety sake and in its place
a single polished metal pipe
set vertical like an insult to gravity and tradition.
I share the grief of ten thousand swallows.

A meeting with fairy-tale actors in the attic of an old school
surrounded by a troupe of life-size puppets
some more real, more interesting, than the people I meet elsewhere.
Several join us for lunch at the vegetarian café
and order nothing more
than soup de jour and toast, a cup of Grimm
with a twist of lemon.

I drive back out of the birthplace of hockey
turn left to a dead end down Old Irishman's Road
retrace my track to Sweet's Corner
a bridge on the St. Croix River
where I can abandon civilization altogether
wade through chest-high sweet summer dykeland grass
descended from the seeds of the Acadians
swept away in the higher tides of Europe's stubborn wars.

The soft stone beneath the grass breeds karst sinkholes
known to grow hungry and swallow Jersey cows.
I step lightly here and hold my arms straight out.
From the road I look like a city fool
pretending he's an airplane

or a clown singing opera in an open field.
I trust the air but not the ground
and at every fifth step feel something like a six-volt thrill of pain
the sting of purple thistle invisible in the timothy.

On the hottest afternoon of the year, I climb the high white cliffs
that crumble like stale bread each time I step
use tree roots for handholds and railings
and pull myself up into the cool shade of the forest
whose floor is cratered from the karst
small dark canyons filling with generations
of pine cones.

Two miles along the escarpment in a sweltering heat
then down to feel the suck of Fundy wind in the estuary
and a tidal field of salt hay
flat and neatly combed by a falling tide
the beautiful hair of all the women on earth.

When the wind stops dead, mosquitoes and black flies
take license to test my sanity.
I fail all the tests, retreat, sprint over cracked glazed mud
curling up into half-formed bowls
jump three snaking brown streams
until
a thunder head appears to the north
as one bull thistle draws fresh blood from my calf
urging me to climb a blue-white gypsum hillside
hunker on a bluff
cradling myself in the roots of a massive pine
my fingers tucked deep into the history of the bark
as thunder fills the valley
slides its broad vernacular into every crevice in these tumbling hills
and fills my head
with wonder.

Insomniac Pier

Soil samples along the Delaware
red tape and ambition
doors opened by the wind
a falcon perched atop three poles lashed into a tripod
the power of rain over art
afternoons like ripe eggplant cradled but not picked
age: two times everything young
she said the weeds own the dawn in Cape Breton
tools, all sharp, available, indigenous
the sound of a young woman singing far off, a honeysuckle throat
thirst tries to be the hero, but fails
falls in with hunger and devotion
a piano in a cold dark room,
voices outside in the snow
a round medallion of quartz
plucked from the shore
tastes like
1964

Home Improvements

when we think about the dead
we improve upon the life they lived
we resurrect their best intentions
smooth over rough circumstance

the invention of video
did certain harm to the departed
although most of us are never truly
ourselves on any camera

the great electronic collective memory
allows some of us to never leave
our interviews carry on past lunch
into generations

the answers are often familiar
since we lack the skills to formulate new questions
the original ones in my profession
are all from the Stone Age
sitting before shadowed cavern walls
asking someone
or himself
who are you?
how did you get here?
where are you going?
what have you had to kill in order to survive?

Full Three Fathoms

Wisdom, elusive as the slipping tide
on cold winter stones encased in ice.
The age of coasts
is proof of another kind of wisdom
beyond my own scud of memory.
Beneath the slate sky
twelve decisions by nine a.m.
Six more before noon
debates and indecisive moments up to three o'clock
followed by sudden conviction.

A cold north wind seeping under the door frame
a flurry of phone calls and confusion
birds asleep by six.
Evenings are ritual and compassion.
There is nothing to report on the ten o'clock news.

For Women Undergoing Mastectomy

Real men continue
to love those whose lives
have been touched by the surgeon's tool.
The beauty of the body
is its ability to adapt.
The beauty of the lover is the same.
Men fight their wars in bars and banks,
trenches and tall buildings.
Women create and fold themselves into our lives
and defend what's left of the world
with secret weapons
found inside their perfect hearts.

A Love of Old Things

There is a love of old things.
Even when they break
they can be fixed
almost always a sense
of wonder built into the basics
of their necessity.

New things are formed
without pretense of a soul
and when they fail
must be replaced
with something even newer.

I am not ashamed
of the sills rotting in my old house
and like a good surgeon
I remove the part of a beam
that has served well
for nearly two centuries.
I carve younger wood
to embrace the old
and foster kinship with ten inch nails.
There is kindness
in the swing of the hammer
its hard-headed kiss
even though the sound of metal hitting home
scares the pigeons from the eaves.

Time itself is an old thing as well
and heals itself
if you are willing to help.
The past we repair
over and over
but today is thrown away
the false expectation that tomorrow
will replace it with something
better.

Going Home
(*with thanks to Alden Nowlan, again*)

I am awake on a summer morning by the clear Atlantic;
the dog is in the kitchen
leaping at the door.
I send her out to bark at the sun
coming up above the steepled spruce.
My wife and children are still asleep
and there is a frame of beauty that surrounds me in the kitchen
where even the caged bird sings.

I am where I want to be
and nowhere else —
that rare sequence of geography and time.
Somewhere, a deep space astronomer
discovers the true centre of things
the origin of the universe:
a man standing in an old farmhouse kitchen,
his hands folded
around a warm cup of tea.

Song of Myself
(for Whitman)

My song is speech,
a chorus of life's culled glossary
for voice to celebrate
all and is.
Far beyond the threads of sinew
that string my words together
there are arms and legs
and sometimes a sensible brain.
I am confused like you and make
a small religion of my dilemma;
I am proud, like you are, over
small victories of making it through
a bad afternoon.

No one but me (and you, of course) is so great
at lamenting one's own diminished deeds
until it all turns into a work of art
as everything should.

I'm drawn into every flame
even the holocaust
but pull back when my eyebrows singe.
I assume, as you assume,
we are all more and less than what appears
but we grow great temperament at green moments:
at the crosswalk standing
with an old woman in a shawl
who knows you;
or at sunrise, standing on
leaves of grass
wearing perfect shrouds of ice.

Orion Keeps Me Honest

Orion keeps me honest —
the old hunter with the squared shoulders
keeps track of how true I am to myself.
He's lost, at times, on the coldest nights
when the north wind conjures up the camouflage
of the great milky wash of stars
but usually Orion stares down
at me
when I forget just where I am
or why.
My daughter, at three, renamed the hunter
O'Brien
and refused to believe he ever killed anything,
Greek or Irish, of this earth or in the sky.
If constellations have souls
then Orion's is large, expansive and light — a vapour of good will.
His hunting is all behind him now
and he's a vegetarian like me.
We know there are many different breeds of warriors.
Some find kindness to be a worthy grenade
against every foe.
The sky is filled with every sort:
some stars point us north or south
some scramble east to west.
These days Orion seems to be content
to station there
beyond my back door
and when he sees us emerge
on a frozen night
pretends we are something immortal
speaks caution to the wind
and spreads the rumour to all the other gods
in the neighbourhood.

The Middle Ground
(*For John and Dominique*)

Claude Monet did not paint the object
but the space between the viewer and the thing observed.
Like him my job is to perceive invisible worlds
between
here and there
and write it down
like this,
this middle ground between
the poet and the poem,
a life lived in dreamy air
separating me from
hard objects of reality.
It means I get to leave my body,
swim out through my eyes
and breathe the light
until I've lost my name
in favour of the subtle now
of becoming
another settled immigrant in the sea
of thirsty air.

On the Air:
WECU Radio, Greenville, North Carolina, 1970

I'm all alone, near midnight
playing Moby Grape, Jefferson Airplane,
Hendrix and cuing up Quicksilver Messenger Service,
my voice in between the music attempting to scratch away
at small truths.
Near certain that no one is listening
I'm talking to myself in the Tarheel South as usual.
I launch into a tirade against the war (why not?),
all wars in fact,
and suddenly the board lights up.
I give way to Grateful Dead
and pick up the phone and listen to
a college girl
whose boyfriend has died in a motorcycle accident.
She's crying now and cursing too
because she had convinced him to go to school,
avoid the draft
and now he's dead —
her fault
and mine too, somehow.

Before I say I'm sorry,
the door bursts open
and three brutes appear,
three redneck jocks, each the size of bulls,
all Budweiser of breath.
They heard my soliloquy,
stand sucking air
with bleary eyes intent
on defence of holy wars.

I say goodbye to the sorrow on the phone
as the record needle is scored across the Dead
broadcasting a great skid of vinyl into the void
just before
three patriots announce my punishment.
When the first one grabs my throat
I flick the toggle on the mic
and a small North Carolina audience hears
the sound
of what's left of America
gasping for air.

Tornado Outside DisneyWorld

Go back to sleep,
it's only the wind,
I tell my daughter
that night in St. Cloud
while outside
the black vortex sweeps by
and in the morning we see orange trees ripped from the earth,
their surprised roots still shaking at the sky.
Sleepers have been sucked from mobile homes
and drawn up into the wind.
Some land on the hoods of cars
driving south on the Florida Turnpike.
A baby is found on a mattress in the arms of an oak tree —
alive, somehow immune to violent shifts of seas of air.

And how to explain to my own child
how wrong adults can be,
how little we really comprehend our world,
our great foolish faith in
logic and truth,
our complex mythology of
finding narrow paths
between chance and consequence.

A Small Sad Dog in Paris

Last night I found a Mercedes hubcap
and carried it all the way to the Arc de Triomphe
then I left it like a supplicant at the doors of Gucci.
Near midnight we walked the Champs d'Elysee
for twelve cold blocks
before the avenue grew weary
of our talk of poetry
and it ushered us into a black taxi
with the surly driver
who wore his arrogance like a uniform.

I slept well at Les Argonauts Hotel
despite the obligatory smashing of dishes
on the doorsill of the Greek restaurant downstairs.
The next day I trekked through centuries of art
at the Louvre in twenty minutes —
the Mona Lisa in her melancholy glass prison
did not recognize me in the Oriental crowd
but I waved anyway.

At the Salon du Livre,
I read poetry out loud to an unsuspecting crowd
convincing half of Europe
that Canadians were either bold, or proud, or lunatic.
In search of my uncle's billet during the war,
I discovered it was now a private school for girls
and asked a woman to take my picture
by the door.
I tried to smile
while she did the deed, as if by threat,
then slapped the camera back in my hand and ran,
her hands clutching at her purse
like she was choking a bird.

I hiked halfway up the stairs of the Eiffel Tower
for what that was worth
in heaving lungs and pounding heart
then wandered into Le Marais and
became lost for hours
until the river found me
and pointed me back towards Notre Dame.
Then just down from Shakespeare and Company
a small, sad dog was
tethered to a lamp post.
Not much is sadder than an old grey poodle
in a hand-knit sweater
waiting outside a café
wagging a cropped tail at strangers
in a city of expensive shoes
and hurried feet.

At the Too Much Hotel in Ottawa
January 13, 2000

I am staying here at someone else's expense
and have too much of everything.
I don't know what to do with it
but there's a large book that I am afraid to open
explaining all the privileges bestowed on me.
There is a small card telling me I can even have
something called a "video breakfast" if I want.
(Do I watch other people eating the food I order
or put my tongue up to the TV and swallow?)

I am concerned the new century will be like this
with too much of everything
and uncertainty at every bite.

I've Always Been Good Friends With My Mind

I've always been good friends with my mind.
We went to school together
and never understood much
but my mind and I
have this binocular relationship
and we share a sense of humour.

My mind is sometimes stronger
but once in a while it acts stupid
because it forgets it has a body
and a soul.

So I get mad and tell my mind
to shut up
and listen to my heart
or even sometimes my feet
until my mind
checks in with the entire anatomy
for news
and boy are we all surprised
because my mind
usually doesn't consult
much with my pancreas,
my ankles or my kneecaps.

Sometimes when I have a lot on my mind
it threatens to go on strike;
already I've offered it a good medical plan
and early retirement,
nostalgia
and flexible hours
but once my mind wanted higher wages
and I asked what it would do with the money.

My mind said it wanted clothes (not anything polyester)
and a new car — a Delorean of all things.
But I invoked my mind's old sometimes-ally
reason
and asked my mind
how he would dress up and drive the Delorean
all by himself.

Then my mind decided it wanted companionship —
it wanted another mind,
a beautiful one to hang around with
because it was getting lonely.
I said I was hurt,
that I always thought it was enough —
just the two of us and all of our appendages.
But no.

My mind was lonely.
It was wasting away in a kind of isolation
I couldn't understand.
I tried to explain
how I would feel with two minds:
one regular, one beautiful,
that maybe it would be crowded or confusing
but my mind was made up.

So I said we would have a trial run.
I'd let a beautiful mind of his choosing
move in — a trial relationship —
and we'd see what happened.

Well, it wasn't that bad
and soon they struck up a bond
and got married as only true minds can
(I was the best man and forgot the ring
but it wasn't my fault
because my mind was so occupied)
and then they started staying up late talking
and I lost a lot of sleep
but they were happy so who was I to interfere?

And now there's talk of children
and I'm worried again
but I'll try to be flexible because the mind, after all,
is a valuable thing
and lately I've been trying to convince myself
that I should change,
I should learn to be something more
than just a prison
for my mind.

Last Will and Testament

To my wife Terry
I give you the square root of sky
the large province of hope
and the view from
the top of the hill at the end of the beach.
I give you finches in the apple tree,
the sunset, west over ice,
the wedge of sunlight in late afternoon
with its warm explosion of colour
at the end of a dark day —
the brooding clouds still overhead,
unable to repress the adventure.

For my daughter Sunyata
I give you every beautiful thing
that ever washed up on our shore,
the remains of glass bottles
sculpted into gems
left lying in the sand on a spring morning.
I give you all lost toys
and the right to re-invent
all worlds to fit your dreams,
newborn pigeons in your cupped hands,
the resurrection of hamsters
and parakeets and dogs.
I give you back all that knowledge and
responsibility has taken away
and so I set you free.

For Pamela my youngest daughter,
I give you a room full of balloons.
I give you the chocolate from the tops of
all the donuts at the Halifax airport restaurant
and I also give you balance —
the ability to walk with assurance
calmly along any precipice and never look down.
I give you solid footing with each step
and guardians
in the form of wind and snow and foam from the sea.
I give you the compass from my desk
and the map I've kept hidden in my heart —
the tools to find the path from despair to happiness
and I will show you how to use them well
and finally this:
the warm wind in your face
as you ride a wild Appaloosa
across a field of clover and Queen Anne's lace;
the solved mystery of being and moving
at once.